ISBN 9781790686438

Front Cover Design by C. Barnes
Book Design by C. Barnes

Printed in the United States of America.

First printed, 2018

DIRT

discover

Directing you to scripture, the pages of "discover" are designed to help you explore. The scriptures provided are the same scriptures that inspired all the other sections of this book. "Discover" invites you to open the Bible, read the scripture verses provided and explore the verses and chapters that surround it, giving you a full experience of scripture. Some "discover" verses are accompanied with wisdom extracted by the Spirit, some are left for you to explore. Use these pages as an exploration of your own spirit, walking the path that the Scripture leads.

inspire

Opening your mind to new and timeless thoughts, the 'inspired' pages will draw you into deep thoughts that have been harvested from scripture or have been exposed through a life spent in the Spirit. These pages are designed to make you think and feel; think through wisdom and how your life can be lived out differently and feel with great emotions the truth and fruit being produced within you as each page is read.

 reflect

Times of great reflection bring about the greatest times of transformation. The pages of "reflect" will bring you to a place where you decide to either grow deeper or continue to remain as you are. Glory comes from a willingness to become transformed into the image of Christ through a reflection on the self. Hard questions will be asked, but these are the questions that mark the turning point of your soul's journey that lead to the greatest glory. Take your time on the "reflect" pages and come back to the questions often. They will become regular visits with yourself so that God's Spirit can intercede and expand you for greater glory.

 talk

The pages of "talk" are yours! They are an invitation for you to talk. Talk through what you're learning, talk through your daily transforming experiences, talk through what has inspired you, talk through the scriptures you discover, talk through it all with God in prayer and praise. Some "talk" pages will direct you to talk through specific questions, while some are left blank. Use these questions and blank spaces to expand your heart, unravel your soul, and become aware of the work God is doing in you.

God Almighty,

I praise you for the ones who open these pages.
I pray that they would feel your presence just as I did in writing these words.
On the days when they are anxious, give them peace.
On the days they are joyful, give them even more joy.
On the days they are suffering, give them rest.
On the days they encounter your Spirit, give them confidence. On the days they feel far from you, illuminate the path back to Christ.

I pray over the Words they Discover in these pages, may they awaken a new depth in their spirit as they encounter Your Word.
I pray over the Inspiration poured out on these pages, may the truth and power of Your wisdom produce a fruitful life in them.
I pray over the times spent in Reflection, may they experience complete joyful surrender and radical transformation.
I pray over the moments they open up their heart and mind to Talk to you, may these moments and days spent Talking be an unburdening and a refreshing.

Father God, I pray they will be changed by your radical Love.
Jesus Christ, I pray they will discover you as a friend.
Holy Spirit of God, I pray they will be empowered and strengthen by Your indwelling presence.

In all things,
Amen

"Relax, everything's going to be alright;
rest, everything's coming together;
open your heart, love is on the way"
Jude v. 2

What are you worried about? What keeps you up at night? What would happen if instead of spending your day in worry and fear, you took time to relax, rest, and open your heart. Read over this verse again and as you do, breathe deeply, reading it slowly another time. Feel your body relax, let your mind rest, and then open your heart and look for love to come your way.

When love is the projected future, hope in the present is felt. If you can see and believe that love is on the way, you can find hope in everything, knowing that as you rest all things will come together to bring even more love and more joy into your open and receiving heart.

when love is in the

future,

hope is in the present

talk

rejoice more

Don't quit when life gets hard, rejoice even more. Your ability to rejoice in all things transforms all things into something to rejoice over.

Inspire

talk

reflection never rejection

Your moments of difficulties, your periods of 'rejection' are not forms of punishments by God, they are opportunities for reflection. Use the question, "why me?" as a reflection not a complaint. Why were you given this opportunity for growth? Why were you chosen to be refined? Why were you stripped down to nothing in order to be built up to something even greater? You will never be rejected by God; you will only ever experience times of reflection.

come back home with praise

All that God does for us is for praise, because praise ushers us Home. He wants us back. He lost us in the beginning and He is doing everything He can to bring us back to Him. Grace on the cross was His biggest move. Our praise for that grace brings us Home, into His arms, back to the beginning. Praise is more than a song or a musical note, it's an escape into God's presence and a coming Home. It awakens our soul to a life in God's embrace.

What can you do to return to God in praise? What would coming Home to God look like for you?

discover

"God's glory is on display in the skies, God's work on exhibit across the horizon. Words aren't heard, voices aren't recorded, but the silence fills the earth: unspoken truth is spoken everywhere. The revelation of God is whole and pulls our lives together."
Psalm 19: 1-2 & 7

God is always on display and always giving a tour of His truth held within the silence of His work. Go, stand outside, look up and in silence let God's work give you a tour of the fullness of His glory. Truth is often not spoken loudly and profoundly, it is often whispered in the silence of your heart. As often as you hear truth spoken loudly from every corner of the world, listen to the silence. As much as you fill your days with noise, fill them with postures of silence. Silence with God is not void of noise, it's full of heavenly praises.

Heaven praises in silence

How have you avoided silence?
What fears do you have about being silent with God?

If you were to sit in silence, what do you think God would say to
you?

talk

talk

Christ illuminates the path of God

The Light of Christ is the illumination of who God is. But the Light is not the destination, it's the illumination. When you seek Jesus, you will be led on a path that is illuminated by His presence. We don't arrive at God and leave it at that. Rather we walk the path that has been illuminated by Jesus.

inspire

talk

The image of God is perfected in you

Who are you? Describe yourself as you would describe a friend. Give details, provide examples, and explore the depths of yourself that only a true friend would know.

....

....

....

....

....

The version of yourself that you are today is not the final destination of who you will always be. God has plans to mature, challenge and grow your self-confidence. God desires to see more joy fill your heart and less fear fill your mind. He has carefully crafted your body, mind and soul to evolve into a holy and glorious being, and He has placed His desires in your heart. Now that you know who you are, who do you want to become?

....

....

....

....

....

....

....

....

....

reflect
R

When you have a sense of where you want to go, you then have to begin to map out the road that will take you there. Think of who you want to become and how you want to live, then answer; What is it that you need to start doing NOW in order to get where you want to go? What practices, mental and spiritual, do you need to incorporate into the rhythm of your life in order to live in such a way that it transforms and transports you into who you want to be?

reflect

talk

prayers are answered in the languages of God

When you pray, do you expect God to answer your prayers in your own language? Of course you do, but have you ever considered learning a new language so that you can hear God's answer clearly, without a language barrier?

I'm not talking about learning a new cultural language, but I am talking about learning the language of God. To think God only speaks one cultural language is absurd, but it's also foolish to think God only answers prayers in one love language.

Prayers are always answered; the problem we have is that we expect them to be answered in the format we desire to receive. God is creative, which means the answers to your prayers require you to get creative as well. Explore a new way of receiving answers, new ways of experiencing God...learn a new language of God.

inspire

Explore new and creative ways of hearing from and speaking to God:

Worship in song
Take a day of solitude (alone time!)
Fast with the intent to let your hunger become a hunger for God
Listen to friends or counsel from someone you trust
Read Scripture praying for the Spirit to reveal truth
Meditate in prayer, song, silence, or over scripture
Get outside and let God's creation speak
Reflect on the patterns of your life, examine your days to see how God is creating a pattern
Practice generosity
Creatively let God move through you (paint, craft, write)

discover

"Everything comes from Him;
Everything happens through Him;
Everything ends up in Him.
Always glory! Always praise!
Yes. Yes. Yes!"
Romans 11: 36

Beginning, middle, and end, all is wrapped up in God's design and purpose. He doesn't just get everything started, He brings it full to the end, creating a bond with you along the way. It can be hard to imagine that all things, good and bad, are wrapped up in a gracious God. Disaster never comes from God, but the beginning of redemption always does. As soon as the struggle starts, God begins His plan to connect to, strengthen, and empower you. He is the first responder to all disasters, on the front line of every battle, ready to bring all things to Him in the end.

God is the first responder to disaster and the finisher of all good things

talk

love is the answer

love is the purpose

The universe would agree; love is always the answer. Everything in life comes with the purpose of transforming you to love more and more. The most impressive transformations happen when you can accept everything as a chance to be love or become loved.

What do you need to accept as an opportunity to expand in love?

discover

"Here's what to do, God helping you: Take your everyday, ordinary life- your sleeping, eating, going to work, and walking around life- and place it before God as an offering. Embracing what God does for you is the best thing you can do for Him."
Romans 12:1-2

The only difference between an ordinary life and a glorious life is awareness. Awareness allows you to see God as He works in the ordinary moments of your life and gives you the right amount of pause to extend those moments in worship. When you go from ordinary to awareness to worship, you transcend into a new way of living and you end up embracing God in each moment. This is true worship; through a greater awareness, embrace God in everyday ordinary moments.

awareness of God

in ordinary things

brings glory

to ordinary things

Heighten your awareness of God; over the next few days, record and write through the moments when you were able to recognize God as well as the moments where you lacked awareness of God.

talk

talk

Praise God even if...

Praise God even if it doesn't make sense.
Praise God even if it's hard.
Praise God even if there is no joy.
Praise God even if I don't know what to do.
Praise God even if I am afraid.
Praise God even if I don't know why.

(fill in the blanks with the things in your life that are hard to praise God for; praise Him even if)

I will praise God even if....

_____

_____

_____

_____

_____

_____

_____

_____

_____

_____

_____

_____

_____

_____

reflect

accept what is given

move forward in hope

Wanting separates you from God's desire to give you all that you need. Don't spend your days living in constant wanting, accept what has come, see the blessing it is, and move forward with hope. Having desires is to be human, but having too many strong wants distracts you from enjoying the simple presence of God. All you need has been provided, all your desires are met in Him.

inspire

to praise &
to discover
God

Good things come so that we can praise God,
bad things come so that we can discover God.

inspire

talk

Three in One

What do you really want from God?

_____
_____
_____

How would you introduce Jesus to others if He were a friend?

_____
_____
_____
_____

Who is the Holy Spirit?
> *Sit for a moment in silence and breathe as if every inhale is an inhale of the Spirit of God and every exhale is the letting go of all thought. When another thought enters, simply breathe it out and inhale the Spirit of God.*

After a few minutes, journal how you felt connecting your breath to the Spirit of God.

_____
_____
_____
_____
_____
_____
_____
_____

reflect

talk

"Live a lover's life, a life Jesus would be proud of: bountiful in fruits from the spirit, making Jesus attractive to all, getting everyone involved in glory & praise."
Philippians 1:11

Making Jesus attractive is living like Jesus, not screaming, preaching and yelling about the religious Jesus we think we know. Jesus was loved by many, yet we find ourselves in a world today where Jesus followers are hated. We have stopped being attractive and have become annoying. Live a lover's life, a life focused on being in love with life and with Jesus, passionate about loving others and devoted to bringing all glory & praise to Jesus.

a lover's life is attractive because love is the most attractive attribute of the soul

talk

Transformed for eternity

I would rather rely on God to bring about lasting transformation than rely on myself to bring about temporary satisfaction. Too often, in my own strength and determination, I seek the temporary satisfaction, ignoring the opportunity to be transformed for eternity.

inspire

What pleasure or satisfaction do you need to let go of in order to
be transformed?

"Reaching out for Christ, who has so wondrously reached out for me. Friends- I've got my eye on the goal, where God is beckoning us onward to Jesus. I'm off and running and I'm not turning back. So let's keep focused on that goal, those of us who want everything God has for us."
Philippians 3:12-14

When you reach for Christ you will find that He was already reaching for you, He was already extending a hand from Heaven. If the goal of the human soul is Heaven, then we must fix our gaze on heaven-bound things. And not just looking towards Heaven waiting and wondering, rather running in the direction our eyes take us. That's the thing about life; wherever your eyes are gazing, your feet will follow. Have a single focus on Jesus and your feet will run in His direction.

where your eyes look

your feet will follow

What is distracting you from the grace of Christ? How can you begin to run in His heaven-bound direction?

talk

There is never a moment that God isn't working in your favor for your eternal being.

inspire

talk

gifted out of Grace

No matter how much I try to 'obey' or follow a pattern of 'rules', healing will always be a gift, not a rewarded. We are not rewarded for good behavior; we are gifted out of grace. The gift you desire to receive from God comes when you begin to realize you are not in control of the blessings. Blessings and gifts are given through grace, not rewarded through obedience.

talk

life without love is death

Life is comprised of moments of love. From love you were created and from love you receive life. We need love to survive, even science proves that love and kindness brings more life than water and sunlight.

Imagine a world without love, would we even exist? Life without love is death. Death is not a lack of health, it's a lack of love.

Love must be given and received. If it ceases to be given, it will no longer come to be received. When love is exchanged between two life forms, life is created. When love is withheld between two life forms, death begins its work.

Think about the cross of Jesus. It was the place where death was conquered. But how was it conquered? It was not power or force. It was not fought. It was overcome with love. Jesus beat death through love. The love He received from the Father and the love He gave the world transformed a cross of death into a resurrection to life.

Acts of love like Jesus' greatest sacrifice will save the world from death. Great moments of love will save the world. If we all lived our days with the intention to love, we could change the world. If we chose to love, even if it meant being uncomfortable or taking chances, we would be saving the world.

inspire

talk

To love & be loved

Jesus' greatest mission was to give love to the world, but He also spent time receiving love as well. He would extend the gift of love to many, but we can see that He also had relationships that were allowing Him to receive love. As much as He gave, He also needed to receive. Your life is dependent upon such things as well; the ability give love abundantly and the strength and courage to give love unconditionally.

In what ways are you most able to give love?

_____

_____

_____

In what ways are you most able to receive love?

_____

_____

_____

What is the greatest moment of love you have experienced in your life?

_____

_____

_____

_____

reflect

talk

"Pursue the things over which Christ presides. Don't shuffle along, eyes on the ground, absorbed with the things right in front of you. Look up, be alert to what is going on around Christ- that's where the action is. See things from Christ's perspective."
Colossians 3:1-2

see things from

Christ's perspective

praise
is communion with God

God's greatest desire is praise. As much as He enjoys the good deeds you do honoring Him. As much as He applauds your honesty and integrity. As much as He loves your 'obedience'. And as much as He enjoys your prayers and petitions. His greatest desire is for you to praise Him.

This is not a boastful request, for God does not fall into pride and selfishness. He is not asking for praise so that He can feel good or be given all the attention. And He is certainly not lacking in anything. Rather, God's desire for you to praise Him is all about you.

When you enter into moments of praise, God receives honor, but what you receive is even greater. To praise is to rest. To praise is to feel peace. To praise is live in joy. To praise is to eliminate worry and fear. To praise is to experience great amounts of energy flowing through you.

Praise sets your spirit in line with the Spirit of God and provides you with a glimpse of heaven. It places you in a posture that is able to give and receive love. Praise is the ultimate and highest form of connection to God. for to praise God is to be connected to His Spirit of praise and worship.

God is not boastful and does not need our praise, rather the opposite is true. We are boastful and need praise to set us free from the pride and selfishness that damages our spirits. Praise aligns the spirit of the human soul with the Spirit of the Living God. Praise is the gateway to heaven. Praise is God's greatest desire, because praise is His favorite way of communing with you.

Inspire

Write your own psalm (song) of praise. If God were standing before you, how would you praise Him?

talk

talk

love deeply, be a friend, discover beauty

"Go ahead and be what you were made to be:

1. *Without enviously or pridefully comparing yourself with others, or trying to be something you are not.*
2. *Love from the center of who you are, don't fake it.*
3. *Be good friends who love deeply*
4. *Don't burn out; keep yourselves fueled and aflame.*
5. *Don't quit in hard times, pray harder and be cheerfully expectant.*
6. *Make friends with nobodies.*
7. *Don't hit back.*
8. *Discover beauty in everyone."*

Romans 12: 4-19

Which of these 8 virtues do you excel in practicing in your daily life?

....

....

....

Which of these 8 virtues do you need to practice more in your life?

....

....

....

reflect

What can you do today to emphasize what you are confident in doing, and what can you do today to strengthen what you need to improve?

"If I keep my eyes on God, I won't trip over my own feet."
Psalm 25:15

The reason you feel like life keeps tripping you up and giving your bruises, is because you're looking at the world around you, instead of the One who designed the world. Keep your eyes on God and you won't have to worry about your stumbling. Bruises are evidence of a life lived in distraction. Keep your eyes focused on God and the path you walk will be paved with glory. There is no guarantee the path will all be downhill, but the uphill grade God gives you, simply strengthens you and prepares you for greater glory.

stay focused,

eyes wide open

Talk

manifest the Spirit of God within you

Do you wish there was more joy in your life?
Do you wish you were loved?
Do you wish you were successful?
Do you wish you were brave?

Then be filled with joy, love everyone you meet, be confident enough to hold success, and choose to be brave. Whatever you wish to see in yourself, be it! God has not given you a Spirit of fear, which means He has given you a Spirit that is full of joy, love, success, and confidence.

Manifest the Spirit of God within in you, which is to say that the Spirit is already within you. You don't need to ask for joy, you need to be the joy. You don't need to pray for others to love you, you need to be the love. You don't need to pray for success, you need to build it. You don't need to pray to be brave, you need to place yourself in situations that require great amounts of bravery.

We often take the power of the Spirit to only be effective in 'spiritual' things, but the Spirit is alive and active, ready to manifest all that you desire from within you. It never comes from the outside, all power and joy from the Spirit comes from within.

Inspire

What do you need to be? What strength of the Spirit do you need to manifest within you so that it can transform the things around you?

If you have experienced any type of indwelling love, joy, peace, patience, forgiveness, or grace, then you have manifested the Spirit of God. How have you experienced the manifestation of the Spirit in you throughout your life?

talk

you are

eternally blessed

now

Eternal life is more than 'living forever', it is living abundantly now. Eternal life starts in the now and extends into eternity, which means the now has a significant impact on the direction that your eternal life flows. Jesus died for life now and forever, but if you only hope in the forever, you reject the life He offers you now. Live now as if it were eternally blessed, because it is.

Inspire

talk

discover

"Your life is a journey you must travel with a deep consciousness of God" 1 Peter 1:18

Have you noticed God lately? Have you really stopped to look for God?

Your life is comprised of moments in which God is present, active and fierce. But are you living consciously of it? Or do you find yourself unconscious when it comes to the things of God?

Have you been knocked out by hate, fear, and busyness? Do you spend your days drifting through life, unaware of a very obvious and present God?

Take a moment to reflect on your most recent memories...do you see goodness in them? Reflect on your favorite memories...did you feel love, joy or peace? In this moment right now, are you captured by the words of 1 Peter, do you feel them guiding you into awareness?

God never changes, never fades, never forsakes, never abandons, and never takes His eyes off of you, He is infatuated with your everyday life. Become conscious and aware of His gaze.

be aware of the gaze of God fixed upon your face

Talk

the gift of freedom deserves a response

Obedience will never earn you anything, it is a response of gratitude for the gift of freedom. You have been given the gift to freely obey whomever you choose to obey. Obedience to God is the response to the freedom that He has given to you.

Inspire

How have you responded to the freedom God has given you?

_____
_____
_____
_____
_____
_____
_____
_____
_____
_____
_____
_____
_____
_____
_____
_____
_____
_____
_____
_____
_____
_____
_____
_____
_____
_____

talk

wrapped in lovely Things

The background noise of your life significantly impacts the background noise of your thoughts. The sounds, words, songs, and things you look at during the day are subconsciously filed into your mind and spirit and are played on repeat. These repeated thoughts form the reality of your life. The more your mind and spirit wraps itself around negative thoughts and feelings, the more your life becomes consumed with experiencing these feelings. However, the more your mind and spirit wraps itself around good and Godly thoughts and feelings, the more your life becomes consumed with seeing good in all things.

What can you listen to daily to develop a positive mind?

_____

_____

_____

_____

_____

What can you look at daily to develop a clear image of what joy in Christ looks like?

_____

_____

_____

_____

_____

reflect

What do you think about yourself? What words are you saying to yourself every day? Are they words of encouragement or always words of criticism?

_____

_____

_____

_____

_____

_____

_____

_____

Write a list of positive affirmations about you and your life, wrapping your mind and spirit in uplifting and lovely words, creating a background noise that is a song of glory instead of a sound of disaster.

_____

_____

_____

_____

_____

_____

_____

_____

_____

_____

_____

_____

reflect

update the status of
your relationship with God

"When you call on me, when you come and pray to me, I will listen.
When you come looking for me, you'll find me. When you get serious about finding me and want it more than anything else, I'll make sure you won't be disappointed."
Jeremiah 29:12-13

Go read Jeremiah 29:11, and you will be filled with great hope for the future, but don't stop there, there's always more. Jeremiah delivers a message from God and the whole message offers more than just hope for the future, it gives insight into the present status of your relationship with God.

God promised a hopeful future, good plans and prosperous things, but then God gave some directions, not a formula of sorts to get the prosperous life, but the relationship piece essential to receiving and perceiving a prosperous life. God says, when we get serious about our relationship with Him, we'll never be disappointed, and this is for two reasons. First, a pursuit of God is your spirit's designed purpose. When you seek God, your spirit is awakened and given life. Second, a serious relationship with God is mutual. As you become infatuated with God, you find that He is head-over-heels for you, completely obsessed and over the moon in love with you. Your 'getting serious' status with God is what makes the present life delightful and the future eternal life hopeful.

How can you begin to enter into a more serious relationship with God?

talk

discover

*"Stop doubting & just believe. Blessed is the one who believes but
has not seen proof."*
John 20:30

Insane amounts of courage come from the moments you just decide
to believe. Doubts are natural, they happen, but they do not rule
over you. Doubts are a gift, for they point to the place where belief
can overcome...but only if you choose to believe without proof. If
you doubt God, don't search for proof, search for Him.

if you doubt God,

don't search for proof,

search for Him

What doubts have you had about God? How have you doubted God's abilities or character? If you were to meet God, would you still hold your doubts?

talk

let God initiate a

surprise

Stop controlling and manipulating your life, let God surprise you. Of course, you need to take action and to create movement, but never become so fixated on controlling the outcome that you leave God's creative power out of the journey. Sometimes, the work is best completed when God initiates a surprise.

inspire

talk

from limitations to

limitless

Limitations are often seen as weaknesses, and weaknesses are often handed over and credited to the work of evil. But the redeeming God takes what seems to be a limitation and brings it into the light of truth so that the same limitation that once brought sorrow and pain, can now bring joy and purpose.

talk

Gratitude creates value

Without gratitude, life would be cease to hold value. Life is not measured in moments, but rather in moments that are captured and held on to with love.

Create a gratitude list beginning with the things you are most grateful for about yourself, then moving into the things you are grateful for about your life, and ending with the things you are most grateful for that you know without a doubt God has provided for you to enjoy.

reflect

Talk

"Be strong. Don't give up! Expect God to get here soon." Psalm 31:24

Expectancy is the greatest posture to hold when blessing is around the corner. In the same way, expectations will always prevent you from seeing the blessing that is already around you. Don't ever give up on being expectant; remain pregnant with joy and hope. God is always around the corner.

pregnant with joy,

expecting new hope

talk

weaknesses point to an opportunity for a holy strength to redeem

Sometimes we need to be set free from our limiting beliefs about the weaknesses we hold on to. We need to be given permission to see our weakness not as a limitation but rather as an opportunity to discover great strength. Let your heart and mind shift from limitation to liberation, from fear to faith, and accept the gift of weaknesses. Your weakness is a badge of honor when it can become a source of greater, holy strength.

Inspire

What weaknesses do you recognize in yourself? How can God create a greater strength in you from within your weakness?

talk

wholeness is greater than fullness

An answered prayer is meant for your wholeness not your fullness. If you find yourself praying for that which will satisfy you in this moment, you are seeking a god of magic and not a God of mercy. God is more concerned with your wholeness, not your fullness.

talk

proclaim truth not lack

Think deeply about what you really want, the deepest desire of your soul. Do you want to be successful? Do you want to be happy? Do you want to go on vacations? Do you want to write a book? Do you want to fly a plane? Whatever it is that you want, turn it into a reality by proclaiming it as a statement. You don't want to be successful, you are successful. You don't want to be happy, you are happy. Whatever you want, make it a true statement and write it over and over, filling these next few pages with words of proclamation.

inspire

Talk

talk

all moments are in need of love, forgiveness, peace, & Thankfulness

Life starts to make sense when you adopt the perspective of Jesus. You will see all of life as moments that are in need of love, forgiveness, peace, & thankfulness.

inspire

talk

"There has never been the slightest doubt in my mind that the God who started this great work in you would keep at it and bring it to a flourishing finish in the end."
Philippians 1:6

Your entire life is a continual buildup of growth into your final 'being'; an eternal mind & an awakened spirit. There is never a moment that God isn't working in your favor for your eternal being. God keeps growing you, keeps pushing you to new strengths, keeps challenging you to new heights, keeps loving you to new depths, keeps working in your favor so that you can come to be a mature, eternal and awakened being.

God keeps

working

evolution is necessary

for survival

God leads us into new directions, pushes us into hard situations, and guides us down uncomfortable & unfamiliar roads so that we are transformed into evolved beings. Evolution is necessary to survive, and evolution of the soul is always a result of being forced to adapt and thrive beyond what we could handle before.

Inspire

talk

God is alive within us

If God is alive in us, then our purpose is to keep Him alive! If we neglect the Spirit, we strangle and suffocate the Spirit of God. If we ignore the Spirit, we extinguish the Spirit's influence in the life and world we live in. How often have you found yourself having to choose between your desires and the promptings of something deep within you? How many times have you felt a pull towards something different and strange but ignored it because you were afraid? How often do you ignore conversations about the Spirit of God because you worry about what others might think of you? Friends, you are suffocating the Spirit of God. He lives and moves in you, not around you. The Spirit is not a floating being in the world, it is alive in you; you are the host and the Spirit will die if you continue to ignore it's daily guidance.

What do you feel the Spirit has been trying to do in you, through you and with you?

....

....

....

....

....

reflect

Are you ready to give life to the Spirit within you and A.C.T. (act, confess, or transform) on these promptings? What A.C.T.s can you do to bring the Spirit back to life in you?

reflect

overcome doubt and

overcome the world

Doubt is not the antithesis of faith and you should never be ashamed of experiencing doubt. But the doubts you carry around in your head are holding you back from believing the truth about yourself. Your doubts are paralyzing you. Accept the doubt as something you experience but never let the doubts you feel define who you are. Overcome doubt and you can overcome the world.

Inspire

What doubts do you have about yourself?
What do you need God to say to you to help you overcome these doubts?

talk

from pride to forgiveness

When do you feel the most pride?

_____
_____
_____
_____

Where are you being dishonest with yourself, with God, or with others??

_____
_____
_____
_____

If you were to humble yourself, who would you forgive first and what would you say?

_____
_____
_____
_____
_____

reflect

talk

bring glory

here and now

Believe that glory is coming, that is what hope is for. But do not neglect your role in bringing glory into the present. We are called to be carriers of glory, which means as much as we believe and hope for glory to come raining down upon us we also must take the same amount of strength and desire into bringing glory to the One who will bring all things into glory in the end. Glory surrounds you, capture it and carry it with you, explore its depths so that you can be exalted in greater, ever-increasing glory.

Inspire

talk

hand delivered

holy weapons

God does not fight the battle for you, He hand delivers the weapons you need to fight. He personally meets you on the battle field and equips you with all that you need to fight. This means, you are going to have to fight. Be a warrior armed with the weapons of God, ready to fight with love, peace, justice, hope and joy.

Inspire

talk

"God is educating you; that's why you must never drop out. This trouble you're in isn't punishment; it's training, the normal experience of a child of God. God is doing what is best for us, training us to live out God's holy and best. Later, of course, it pays off, for it's the well-trained who find themselves mature in their relationship with God."
Hebrews 12:7-11

When troubles comes, accept them as training. Troubles are an opportunity to be trained by God to live a holy life. Holiness is not an easy process, it's a masterclass in becoming more like Jesus. As a child of God, Jesus received the utmost training, which ultimately required Him to die on the cross. You can consider it an honor to receive the same training Jesus received, for this is the training that will produce a Christ-like heart and spirit in you.

Trained like Christ,

To be like Christ

talk

faith stands on the promises of God

Faith takes risks and actions that are based on the promises of God. The promises of God are the destination; faith is the journey needed to get there. When you know and believe in the promises of God, you can move forward in faith. God promises to love you, that is enough of a reason to do all things in faith.

Inspire

What promises of God can you commit to faithfully believing?

talk

be honest with God

Are you honest with God or are you too concerned with being holy and proper in His presence?

Be raw. Be honest. Be angry. Be scared. Be open. Be truthful. Be disappointed. Be sad.
Be what you need to be before God, He welcomes it, but be prepared because He will transform it.

If you never brought your fear God
how could ever He turn it into faith?
If you never brought your doubts before God
how could He turn it into belief?
If you never brought my anger before God
how could He turn it into joy?
If you never bought your sadness before God
how could He turn it into dancing?

Inspire

Be honest with God. Unburden all things on this page.

talk

a love letter

Write a love letter from God to you. Imagine what He might be saying to you. Remember, this is a love letter, it's not a list of disappointments you might be thinking God is compiling against you. Write a letter using words that you desire to hear spoken over you.

reflect

aggressive

forgiveness

Grace is the aggressive forgiveness of God that bridges the gap between us and Him. Grace makes communion with God possible.

talk

silent before God

"Go, stand on the mountain at attention before God.
God will pass by you."
1 Kings 19:11-12

When you're ready to hear from God, and willing to listen with the intent to follow, you must be content with hearing a whisper. Not a large forceful wind, that would be too obvious. Not from an earthquake, that would cause a scene for everyone. Not from a fire burning, that would bring upon disaster. God's gentle & quite whisper is easily heard when you make the trip to the Mountain— *hint,* you have to set a part a specific time and place, completely separate and holy, for the purpose of positioning yourself to hear a whisper.

What ways have you been expecting God to speak to you?

What separate and holy place can you create and go to in order to hear from God in a whisper?

How can you make it a priority to go to your 'mountain top' place more consistently (daily, weekly, annually)?

R reflect

God can always be found, because He is hidden in everything

When you look for God, He can always be found. This is a fact. No matter how you look, where you search, or who you are as you look, God is found. The problem we face is not that God is missing from our view, but rather that our eyes have been covered with the blur of a false sense of God. God, full of love and grace, is not hard to find. But the god you seek is not always the same God who exists. Are you looking for a god who delivers a wish? Are you looking for a god who makes life easy? Are you looking for a god or do you seek God?

God can always be found.
When you get serious about finding God, you will see He has been hidden in everything. When you want to find God more than you want to find happiness, you will not be disappointed. When you desire God more than you desire to breathe, you will find Him in every breath.

Inspire

talk

The process of joy

Maturity is gained through challenges. Embrace every challenge with joy and consider it pure joy to be invited into the refining process.

Practice seeing your challenges as processes for joy to be made complete in you.

(the challenge) → (the process)

stress from work → I am being challenged and gaining wisdom in my job

financial constraint → I am learning to be content

struggling to become healthy → I am learning to love my body

living a busy lifestyle → I am being given the opportunity to do many things

rocky relationships → I am growing in my ability to love the unlovable

Your turn:

_____ → _____

_____ → _____

_____ → _____

_____ → _____

_____ → _____

_____ → _____

reflect

talk

discover

"I bless God every chance I get;
my lungs expand with praise.
Open your mouth and taste,
open your eyes and see-how good God is.
Blessed are you who run to Him.
Worship God if you want the best;
worship opens doors to all His goodness."
Psalm 34: 1,8-9

Praise God for every moment that is free from pain, fear, and worry and you will find that every moment will become free. Open your mouth and taste how good it is to praise; sing about goodness and you will feel goodness overtake you. It will taste good. Open your eyes to see all that needs praise and you will be delighted to see that there is so much goodness surrounding you. Worship doesn't magically make good things appear, worship simply gives you the perspective of a God who is working all things for good. When you shift your perspective you will taste and see the goodness of God all around you, and all moments will be worthy of praise.

taste & see

the goodness of the Lord

talk

135

surrender to what is

best

Every step you take towards a goal needs to be followed by an equal force of surrender. Surrender removes your desires from the action and places you in the position to receive what is best.

Inspire

talk

create with the

Creator

God calls you His child, which means you have inherited the great honor of being a co-creator in the work of His Spirit. This is an honor and a responsibility.

As a co-creator, you have the Spirit infused power to create more love, more faith, more grace, more hope and so much more in this world. As often as you ask God to deliver and create these things in your life, take your place as co-creator and create from within.

The Spirit of God lives within you, you have been given all the power and strength you need to co-create with God.

Create love.
Create joy.
Create happiness.
Create peace.
Create hope.
Create more and
more will be created
from within.

Inspire

praise, pray, & worship

Repeat

How do you focus on God when the chaos of life ensures that silence is lost and peace is forgotten? Establish the practice of a "Breath Prayer." Set to the rhythm of your breathing, these short and simple prayers become a new path for your spirit to follow when chaos endures; they direct your heart back onto God in the subconscious thoughts of your daily life. Think of the normal paths your spirit and mind take during the course of a day, do they take you on thought paths of "I am not good enough", "I am weak", "I am tried", "I am afraid", "everything is wrong", "everyone is out to hurt me"?

If you read through the Psalms you will certainly find that David's mind wondered down these paths too, but he was quick to fight back with praise and change the path from depression to joy, from despair to hope, and from great amounts sorrow to great amounts of dancing.

His secret is simple, rejoice over and over, worship God and repeat. He knew that the path of despair was not a path that God was going to be found on, so he stood up and praised in simple words and in a simple tune. Breath prayers are a way of finding your way back to God when you've been unknowingly lost and wondering.

Develop your own breath prayers; the short, simple, repeatable phrases that can become the mantra that plays on repeat in your mind all day. Reprogram the mind to say and believe what the Spirit is already speaking over you.

reflect

breath prayers

(inhale)… (exhale)
"Jesus, I need you"
"My God, is close to me"
"Speak Lord, I am listening"
"God is with me, God is for me"
"Your will, be done"
"Come Jesus, Come"
"I am, completely loved"
"You, are a good Father"
"I am forgiven"
"He is doing, new things in me"
"I believe, good glory is here"
"My God, is present"
"God, wants to satisfy me."
"I am, one with Christ"
"God can do miracles"
"God is real"
"Abba, be close to me"
"I am covered, in grace"
"I am filled, with joy"

Write your own breath prayers or create repeatable mantras that can calm and guide your spirit back to God. Create your go-to thoughts of truth and peace for times of stress and chaos.

talk

"Thy will be done"

When God placed a purpose on your life, it wasn't a question of WILL you do it? No! It was a question of WHEN will He do it through you?

it will be done

"Thy will be done"

When God placed a purpose on your life, it wasn't a question of WILL you do it? No! It was a question of WHEN will He do it through you?

it will be done

"Shout Hallelujah! Give glory!
Adore Him.
He has never let you down,
never looked the other way.
He has never wandered off,
He has been right there listening.
Coming back to their senses,
people are running back to God."
Psalm 22:22-27

No life on this earth is devoid of God's handiwork, simply put; your perception is misleading you to believe only what you see. When in despair, focus on the truth that has marked your life with the hand of God. Look back and see what you may have missed before, He has been there all along, open your eyes and mind to see, come back to your sense of God.

remember when, and

remember Who

To rest is to worship

Rest is an act of worship. Rest is a time of trusting. To enter into rest is to cease striving, to cease controlling and to begin to learn the rhythms of trust and surrender in God. If you can trust God, you can rest. If you can rest, you are trusting that God can handle all things even as you sleep.

Inspire

How can you incorporate more REST into your life?

RELAX (pause and rest the body)

EXPLORE (explore God's word, letting your mind rest from the chatter of thoughts)

SILENT (learn to enjoy and embrace silence)

TIME (cultivate and schedule times of purposeful rest)

talk

shining

brighter and brighter

"Face to face with God, nothing between us and God, our faces shining with the brightness of His face. And so we are transfigured much like the Messiah, our lives gradually becoming brighter and more beautiful as God enters our lives and we become like Him."
2 Corinthian 3:18

How are you becoming more like Jesus?

talk

faith is the

energy of hope

What is faith? Is it saying a prayer and just hoping things turn out ok? Is it looking forward to the future and expecting something good to happen? Is it being able to say "I believe" or is it wishing on a star?

Faith is believing that good things are coming and then choosing to make good things happen. We can wish for things all we want and we can try to have faith it will all eventually work out. Or, we can make it happen using faith as the energy to bring all the anticipation into fullness.

Faith in God is choosing to act like Jesus. It doesn't mean you just hope God does nice things. Faith leads you to believe that you play a very significant role in the outcome of the future and so you choose to love and be kind like Jesus.

Faith is the energy that takes you into perceiving blessing upon blessing.

inspire

talk

Never stop
believing that
good things
are here, and
great things
are coming.

Hope

What good things do you see in your life now? What great things
do you believe are coming?

from fear to

faith

Fear is not the enemy; fear is an opportunity to produce radical faith. Fear becomes the enemy when you let your fear speak louder than your faith. Fear is only the enemy when fear becomes your friend. You can flirt with fear, but don't enter into a relationship. You're already taken.

Inspire

What fears are holding you back from pursuing God greatly?

Write a break up letter with your fears; expose them, letting them
know why you no longer wish to believe in them.

talk

unfolding of the heart

Prayer is not a petition placed before God, prayer is a process of unfolding the heart. Prayer unfolds your heart's desires, places them before God and steps back confidently, knowing very well that the One who holds these prayers is powerful.

talk

159

"We are God's children. We know that when Christ is revealed, we'll see Him and in seeing Him, become like Him-with the glistening purity of Jesus' life as a model for our own."
1 John 2:2-3

glistening like Christ

get through the valley

so that you can

dance on the mountain top

The blessing you are asking for may only be available on the other side of a valley. That valley may include days and months of loneliness, but God never leaves your side. The valley may include moments of deep despair and sadness, but God sings over you moving your feet to dance. The valley may induce wounds, but God is ready to heal and redeem the brokenness. Whatever valley you walk through is simply the journey, it's never meant to be your destination. Get to the other side and you will be able to see more glory from where you stand, because you will see where you have come from and will be able to see the places of great triumph.

inspire

talk

life is measured

in love

What if the length and the joy of your life depended on
how much you loved others?
What if the amount of love you gave to the world was the
same amount of love your received?
What if the value of your life was determined by how much
you gave instead of how much you take?
Love like your life depends upon it. It does.

inspire

adoration is gratitude
for Who not what

Adoration of God is simply holding an attitude of gratitude for who God is, not what He has done for you. Adoring God is being filled with great amounts of joy in each moment, for each moment is held graciously in His presence.

talk

called His child, reflecting His face

How is your life reflecting the unique face of God?

God's glory fills this earth with great amounts of uniqueness, displayed perfectly in the life you live out in the world that surrounds you. To think we are all required to be monks and church leaders is to limit the face of God to one type of lifestyle. God fills the earth with His children, and one of the many inheritances you have received is the greatest honor of displaying His image.

What are the unique gifts and passions you have? What brings you the most joy? When are you most 'creative'?

How would you describe the face of God? This is not the physical face of God, rather the image that His reflects, the persona that He emulates and puts on display for the world to see.

reflect

How can you use your unique gifts and passions to display the face of God in the world you encounter?

reflect

go be &

go tell

Be ready to tell others why you live the way you do. Actually, first, live an astounding and noteworthy life, a life that stands out as being different in love and joy. Then you'll be ready to tell others why. Why do you live joyfully? Why do you smile when the world around you is in tears? Why are you choosing to live the way you do when it's the harder way to live? You live this way because you have discovered that emulating the life of Jesus is the only way to escape death, not physical death but death of the soul.

Inspire

talk

aim your life at God
and you'll never miss
The mark

What is a Christian? Simple, it's a life aimed at God's bullseye. A life that is pointed in the same direction as God's desires for the world. A life that is focused on giving forgiveness, grace, love and compassion. A life that is aimed at what God desires to see in the world. It doesn't mean you always hit the bullseye, for perfection is never the goal. You were simply meant to aim your life in the direction of God's bullseye, and with God's Spirit leading your arrows, you'll never miss the mark.

Inspire

What direction do you feel God is asking you to aim your life?

a spirit refined is a

Spirit of joy

Don't ever jump to the conclusion that God isn't on the job. Instead, be glad that you're in the very thick of what Christ experienced; the spiritual refining process that holds great amounts of glory within. Be assured, the difficulties you experience are not a punishment, they are the gift of being refined like Christ. Be assured, God has not left you on your own, He is working in the difficult moments to refine your spirit so that when glory comes, you can actually perceive it.

What difficulties are you experiencing? How can you see them as refining opportunities? Do you consider it a gift to be refined like Christ?

discover

"God's Spirit is right alongside helping us along.
He knows us far better than we know yourselves. That's why we
can be so sure that every details in our lives of love for God is
worked into something good."
Romans 8:26-28

Because we are fully known by God's Spirit, we can be assured
that He sees the intentions of our hearts and is always working
from within our heart to create a life that reflects those intentions.
A life lived with the intention to love is always worked into
something good; the good of the world in which we daily live.

intended to love

talk

comfort & joy

You are comforted by God, not so that you can be comfortable, but so that you can experience joy in the midst of pain. Comfort comes to bring peace and peace leads us to joy.

inspire

grace is a head on collision with God's embrace

When I throw my weakness into the Lord's greatness, I imagine a head on collision. As my weaknesses are sent heavenward in complete surrender, God's greatness is in pursuit of me in a glorious display, He crashes into me with His grace upon grace. This is the moment and the place in which all my insecurities, failures, and disappointing attempts are overwhelmed by the collision of a Heavenly embrace exploding with Greatness.

Inspire

talk

inhale truth

exhale harm

Inhale the breath of Christ, exhale the doubts.
Inhale the joy of Christ, exhale the fear.
Inhale the peace of Christ, exhale the anxious thoughts.
Inhale the love of Christ, exhale the hate.
Inhale Christ, and let all else fall out of the body.

Inspire

What truths can you inhale as your breathe today? What false and hurtful things can you exhale?

talk

a beacon for prayer,

Jesus guides you from

worry to praise

The antidote to worry is prayer & praise. Worry is the gift of being able to see a need that needs to be covered in prayer. Accept all worry as a beacon for your prayers, then follow the Light that guides you to a safe place. When worry turns into prayer, praise is awakened, your anxious soul starts to remember who Jesus is; the calm peace in the storm, the Light of Hope in your worries, the place of refuge for the weakened. When worry hits, remind your soul who Jesus is and praise Him with all the strength you have left, He will not leave you weak, He will strengthen you with great joy.

inspire

What do you worry about? How can you turn that worry into a prayer?

talk

The rhythm of grace
tells us to float not swim

Imagine being tossed gently by the sea, the water cooling you down and gracefully moving your body across the top of the water. If you were to try and swim, you would get tired and drown. However, if you surrender to the movement of the water and embrace the waves, you will find yourself drifting into the rhythm of grace.

inspire

talk

unleash God

Your prayers are as powerful as your God. If your prayers are small, then God is only expected to do small things. But if your prayers are BOLD, then a big God is unleashed.

Inspire

Write the most BOLD prayers you can think of, challenge God to be a BIG God.

talk

discover

"Go out into the world as a breath of fresh air in this polluted society. Provide people with a glimpse of good living and of the living God. Carry the light-giving message into the night. You'll be living proof."
Philippians 3:15-16

Uncomplicate a life that is following Jesus; be a breath of fresh air to the world, bring light into darkness, and you will be living proof of Jesus. Bring peace where there is none, bring love where hate is abundant, bring hope where fear is overtaking, bring joy where sadness sits.

a fresh breeze of love

cures the fog of hate

talk

what a friend we have in Jesus

Waste potentially productive time with Jesus, that's what friends do. They sit, talk, and do nothing together. They embrace silence when there are burdens. They're the first ones to call when something exciting happens. They choose quality time over tasks and to-do lists. They stay up late chatting. They share their secrets. And most of all, they don't care what they look like when they meet, because they are confident that the love they share is unconditional. Jesus, your friend, doesn't care what you look like,, what you like to do, or how much you can get done...do you care if your friend Jesus doesn't perform miracles, doesn't put on a show for you, doesn't show up in bright lights, and doesn't get anything done...what if He just sat with you and let you chat. Would that be okay?

Inspire

Reflect on the idea of Jesus simply being with you. How would you interact with Him? What would you say to your friend Jesus? Would you be okay with just sitting with a very still and present Jesus?

talk

daily examine

Reflect upon your daily life, daily, and you will see the string of God's Spirit connecting you to your purpose. If you have ever wondered what God has designed you for, practice the daily examine.

At the end of each day;

1. Recall God's presence: Where in your day do you see God's presence? Where in your day did you feel closer to God? Where did you feel far from God? Ask the Holy Spirit to help you to look honestly at your day.

2. Express Gratitude: Think in details—the aroma of coffee brewing, a smile from a co-worker, or a simple sunrise. Recall the gifts that God has given you that you can share with others— your ability to help in a crisis, your sense of humor, or your patience with children.

3. Reflect on your actions: Did you take advantage of the opportunities in your day to express God's love? If you didn't, think about why? If you did, think of how that action leads you to discover your strength and purpose.

4. Notice the patterns: As your review each day, notice the patterns. Where are you seeing more and more of God? What actions are you taking every day that can point to a greater purpose for your life? How can you rearrange your days to focus on these patterns?

5. Hopefulness: End your examine with hopefulness; hope that your attention to your days will produce a Christ-centered spirit in you.

reflect

Practice the Daily Examine:
Recall, Gratitude, Reflect, Patterns, Hope

who have I always been?

The truth about life, the truth about you, is all held within your own soul. You don't need outside assistance to find that which is held within. Deep within you there is truth, the problem you are facing is not who am I created to be, the problem is who have I always been?

inspire

talk

be the proof

Proof is limiting your ability to transform. You're looking for proof that God exists, you're looking for proof that He can do miracles, you're looking for proof that your life will be 'good'. But the proof you are seeking is limiting your ability to become the proof that you need. Often, we find ourselves looking for proof before professing, we need proof before we decide to take action. The truth is that your transformation, your story, is the only proof that will convince your mind and soul to believe. Until you become the proof you need, you will never fully believe.

Inspire

How can you become the proof that transformation and miracles are possible?

live as If your prayers are being answered

Listen to your own prayers. Do you keep praying for the same things? Do you remain focused on what you don't have instead of focusing on what you do have? What would you do if that prayer was answered? If you pray for peace, what would do if that peace already existed within you? If you pray for success, what would you pursue if that prayer was answered? If you pray for healing, who would you be if you were already healed? Live as IF your prayers have already been answered and you may find that the answer was within you the entire time.

Inspire

talk

The prince of Peace is with you

When your heart is aching, the world us upside down, your bruised and beaten from ache and despair. The one thing we need to remember in these moments is peace, yet it's the one thing that escapes from our fragile hands. Thanks be to the God of mercy that He doesn't make us reach in anguish for peace but He comes down in His divine Presence and offers us the Prince of Peace; the one who breathes onto us and speaks "peace be with you".

Stop reaching in your own strength and let Jesus breathe on you in the stillness.

Inspire

talk

a miracle of the heart

The most beautiful miracles happen inside you, instead of in your circumstances. If you receive and hold on to peace, love, or joy, count it as a miracle, because that means God has transformed you.

inspire

God Almighty,

May all that has been written, thought,
or expressed in these pages be transformed
into a greater reflection of you.
Return our spirit often to the places
we have explored.
Lead us to discover more of you.
Teach us to be an inspiration for all.
Allow us to reflect more often.
And give us the greatest desire
to talk to You daily.
Spirit of God, in all that we do,
Remain.
Remain in us as we seek to
Remain in you.

Amen

talk

Made in the USA
Middletown, DE
20 December 2018